Her Own Path:

Poems

Ida VSW Red

Her Own Path: Poems

Pony Paws Press
PO Box 766, Greenfield, MA 01301 USA
averystoicpress@gmail.com

Publisher's Cataloging-in-Publication Data
Red, Ida VSW. Edited by Avery Cassell.

Her Own Path: Poems/Ida VSW Red
ISBN 979-8-9887469-3-5

1. Lesbians – Poetry. 2. American poetry —
Women authors — 21st century. 3. Poetry.

First printing, October 2024
Printed in the United States by Pony Paws Press
Beach photo by Lynn Brown. Back cover photo by
Jeanne Clark
This book would not have been possible without the
vision, care, and stubborn persistence of Ida's
nibling, Avery Garland Cassell.

Ida VSW Red

March 21, 1933 - May 11, 2020

Ida VSW Red: Her Own Path

Ida had a life-long love of words, beginning in her early years as an avid reader in small-town Virginia. She found theater in high school and it remained a constant throughout her life. College and graduate school were devoted to delving into literature in its many forms. As a librarian, teacher, and facilitator of writing groups, she shared the wonder of words with others. She guided many aspiring and experienced writers to use an authentic voice and helped bring out their best. She was proud of her professional work as an editor, polishing the written word to perfection, both for academic and popular audiences.

Despite being a radical lesbian feminist and, for some time, an avowed separatist, she treasured her collection of W. S. Merwin, subject of her Master's thesis and perhaps her first true love in poetry. She was a frequent contributor to *Sinister Wisdom: A Multicultural Lesbian Literary & Art Journal.* While serious poetry was a vessel for her deepest engagement with herself, she also delighted family and friends with her self-described "doggerel" written for special occasions.

Poetry can be a solitary pursuit, but Mothertongue Feminist Theater Collective provided one of her most meaningful experiences of writing and sharing words shaped in community, to both challenge and affirm women's sense of themselves.

Many of the poems chosen by Ida and collected here are highly personal musings on four periods of her life:

- Childhood - age 20, focused on family, loss, and wonder (1933-1954)
- ages 21-42, shaped by marriage, parenthood, and studies in Virginia (1955-1976);
- ages 43-64, embrace of her lesbian identity, divorce, and move to the San Francisco Bay Area (1977-1998); and
- ages 65-84, lastly, the challenges of love, friendship, and aging (1999-2020).

Ida liked to imagine comparing her life trajectory to that of Sylvia Plath. Ida's was perhaps a more mundane and less-heralded life, but one which, thankfully, was long and rich in love and experiences. She chose her own path.

Judith Wood & Becca Knox

Table of Contents

Waking

23 Henry Street
San Francisco, CA

(Steadily) pulsating
Victorian pipes above
staccato cycle in front
idling and revving
counterpoint
asymmetrical mourning
of a single dove
out back

Familiar morning sounds
rusty old rhythms
pausing, moving into
sync with city traffic
failing to mask
the clear strain of
sadness
within

Groundhog Day in the City

Bloody pawprints in soot on white
marble lead from the street
Out back, strays brazen
through the domestic pet door
spraying, wreaking havoc
in the kitchen
endangering the retreat of home

Yep, groundhog sees her shadow
the winter rains go on
Skunk lets loose in your urban patio
Hawk dives past my corporate plateglass
underbelly soft, beak sharply hooked
Groundhog backs into her hole

Please leave warm soft fuzzy
messages on my answering machine
but not too soft, too warm
or I'll feel trapped
expectations looming large
Fix me breakfast just one more time
and I'll be hooked
Cage door clicks shut
all I can do is slam my wings against
the mirror, smashing possibility
No! I'll stay in my hole

"I'm ole miz mole
And I live in a hole
Bless my soul
Love this hole that I live in!"*

Love the toast and
apple-butter, the comfort
want, want, want more
want fiercely, desperately
afraid to go into the light
afraid my shadow side will show
needs sticking out, insistent
sickly white potato sprouts
one from each eye
eyes all over my body

Trying to see beyond the spongy sprouts
trying to see what you see in me
hiding my shadow in dark sweetness
so you'll respond to me, not the sprouts
to me: the me of soft and sharp protections
of beauty and ugliness, boldness and terror
of groundhog habit

coming out of her hole again
in the time between
winter and spring
for one more Groundhog Day

1990

One Sentence

Not a Cause of the Peloponnesian War
For JEW

Sometimes a poem festers
like a fever blister
born of dysfunction
forcing full attention
to a small surface
area throbbing
where the eruption severs
the event from roots and sends
a new form on a swelling course
through sensitive skin to nerve
end and back again, this time
scattering and seeding both surface
and crater with the poem's small
pulsing pain -- feeling's loss
and gain.

1974

Nursery Rhyme

for wps

My father stands
by the swing
pushing me away

Suddenly my canary
and mama and I
on a train sway

Finally with Billy
at grandmama's –
strange new day

New as the library
the rhythm band
mama's job – all from WPA

Daddy stands back
now I swing alone
pumping myself they say

Aftermath

for wms

Grandmama sang to me within big
brother Bill's hearing: "Pony boy
pony boy, won't you be my pony boy?"
somehow convincing a lonely child
far from his father that Santa would
definitely, without a doubt, this
year bring the longed-for steed

He put on a brave front as socks
underwear, comic books and
home-made fudge appeared
said not a word, barely sighed
but in his eighties told me he'd
never gotten over it, never in his life
quite trusted a woman again

2013

Fall

for meu

Smell of dry leaves rushes
me back to pigtail days
raking backyard maple leaves
carrying bushel baskets
of reds, yellows, browns
through the back gate
down three stone steps
to dump by the curb
for our annual bonfire
then up to my room
to knot a bandana
into a hobo sack and out
again on the hunt for a stick
to carry over my shoulder
and several for roasting
weinies and marshmallows

I pass through the kitchen
sniffing baked beans
from the Majestic range
and onions being chopped
Out by the street again
arms flung wide, I jump
into the pile of leaves

from the sidewalk above
as if leaping from a cliff
scattering leaves all over
one perfect red one caught
in a shoelace as I sweep all
the crackling fuel back
into a cone-shaped pile
ready for grandmama's match

2016

Phoebe & Me

for vfu

Each night is a hibernation
morning a slow quickening
as old loves become fast
friends at a distance while
the phoebe returns daily
about the feeder, searching
maybe looking for seeds
a nesting site or a mate
I, meanwhile, without a partner
am fairly well fed & housed
but longing for passion
or close companionship

Is the full moon more desirable
than any of its other phases

If karma believes in me, even
though I don't believe in it

will love evade me now or
could I change my fortune by
licking my thumb & stamping my palm
with each white horse I see
despite mama's commitment to that

superstition but long life without luck

Maybe a loving companion
was not what she desired
unlike phoebe & me

2013

They Met

for vfu + wps

After the blush
a fast cover
Both pause before
eye to eye
leads beyond
lust and fear
to unlikely recognition
Redheaded flapper
makes instant connection
with bad boy artist
They're already running
away from home

2016

Virgin Hemlock I

A child's imagination
slips out the kitchen door
quietly clicks the lattice
gate shut, eyes necessarily
turned back as I move
naturally forward to the
fragrant grasses of Field's
field, attention drawn to
butterfly on fat purple clover
newly brave I steal
down Indian Row
between virgin hemlocks
footfall silent and secure
soft, old brown needles
absorbing all sound save
branching shawls sighing
in waves up heavy trunks
light filtered in narrow
shafts angling questioningly
motes of pollen falling thick
into deep pungent shadow
disturbed by smoke feathers
memory of crisp hot cornpone
mine the smallest special pone
patted into shape by cool hands

big liver-spotted hands hold me
soft, sweet voice reciting
melancholy song of Hiawatha
Pocahontas, Mollie, gone
dark and silent before me
beneath virgin hemlock

Virgin Hemlock II

They say: Pandora
here it is, a gift for you
all yours, but don't, whatever
you do, don't open it!
Of course I do
first, just to take a peek
then to inhale every word
not, as they think
the ills of the world but
dangerous as the plague

I'll grant you - old
wives' tales, sinister
wisdom, bare truths
above all, self-knowledge
Once cracked open
all fly out and in, too
into my center
no boxing it up again
that's for sure. But
he wouldn't understand
the boy with his vanity
ego to be shored up
no matter how many times
the vulture plucks it out

so I just tell him it is
recipes, recipes for pie
since he's so fond of pie
that keeps him occupied
well, that and his rolling
stone and his liver problem
all that takes his attention
while I play with the words
from the book -- oh, yes, it
is a book -- nothing so square
as a box. I begin to rearrange
things just a little. You know,
the mirror a bit to the left
the loveseat at a gay angle
until, really, I have ideas
for a whole other volume
so I get it all down
A New Primer for Women
privately printed in limited
edition, sufficient for all my
women friends and their women friends
until we have everything we need
naturally by ourselves and
enough left over for
sweet talking times and dancing

Virgin Hemlock III

Younger, now that I'm older
running down Indian Row
joy blatant in deep shade
lightly bearing book
and song, memory and line
mask and costume of the
parts I've played -- this
a weight-bearing exercise
said to strengthen the bones
delay the dowager's hump

Between virgin and hemlock
after child, student, wife, mother
comes new time for sisters
and for self integrating all
the parts, shedding skins
saving, showing, saying
only true to me

Grieving soft old hands
cool voice, thin lips
gone before I am ready
leaving heavy mantles
I must alter and wear
brave through sunlit field
under hemlock bough
onto unexplored land

1989

Left Behind

I had a potting bench
built to order with love
just for me facing garden
windows in his spacious
basement workshop, a step
up from grandmama's dark
dirt-covered cellar – hers,
though, lit by glistening jars of
peaches, tomatoes, jellies, juices
filling rough-hewn shelves
to tide us over the winters of
The Great Depression
World War II and beyond

At my lovingly crafted bench
I planned a new L-shaped garden
to start from seed in peat pots
choosing variety, color, size, shape
designing aesthetically pleasing
planting patterns in pencil on a
wooden cheese wheel box top

Six months later, the bed bloomed
gloriously in a riot of beauty
while I moved on to a project

for the garden Club of Virginia
As a new, inexperienced member
I was entrusted only with bulbs
already dried and carefully labeled
for a demonstration bed that I
placed under a pear tree, mixing
brilliant red tulips with the yellow
narcissus and daffodils

These flower beds were almost
harder to leave than the sweet
old family home, two floors and
an attic above the abandoned potting bench

I smuggled one flower
slip across the country
from the old life to the new
a shrimp plant from New
Orleans preserved by my
mother after a '50s visit to
out GI Quonset hut
grad school quarters
where I had tended

the plant a lifetime before
in the happy days
of the marriage I was leaving

The regenerated *Justicia brandegeeana*
still blossoms these many years
later on my retirement home deck
As I start cuttings for my daughters
I am caught by layered memories
of the many gardens and
relationships I've created
nurtured, left or changed

2013

Peace on May Day

in midlife, longing
for a new life, still
taking care of an
old life, looking
for a symbol, a sign

my children raided the
porch boxes of new yellow
pansies, 2" wide, 2" high
my lover sent classic long-
stemmed pink rose buds

determined to fit all
into a curved arrangement
but not seeing how, I
wandered into my back
yard to find the first
rose of the season already
swollen, a huge moon

an old variety, the Peace
Rose refuses to be
faithful to pink or yellow
subtly blending both into
its fragrant blossom

open wide to the elements
yet holding its shape
long after "full-blown"

placed in the center
the single Peace Rose
pulled the pink buds
and the yellow faces
into absolute harmony
soothing me into belief
again in possibility

if the warring voices within
can thus find their balance
cannot all extremists open to
each other on middle ground?

1986

Rabbit

Silent -- so silent
and still, deathly still
is one way to survive

Let the sharp-beaked
ones miss me altogether as I
blend into the bush

Stay brown, stay alert
don't make a sound
feeding, mating, bearing
oh, bearing the young

Let them be, knowing
I cannot protect them
far beyond our nest
and then only for a while

Leave them on their own
in harm's way
trusting they already
know how to survive

Silent and still in the open
soft and trusting, all in a
heap with their sisters
safe in dark retreat

1996

Heartwood

In a sudden rain shower
the distant sun disk
drops from a black
cloud, streaking brilliance
along the horizon while
the excitement of little birds
draws attention
to nearby woods
jarred by loud
knocking, drilling
a flash of long wings
at a snag where
a crimson crest
seems to radiate
redder than red

The tall pileated
woodpecker knocks off
bark in great sheets
the way certain women
catch all eyes
drown out the chatter
make instant shamble
of loyalty + commitments
lay bare raw desire

2014

Synesthesia Cycle I

Imagining a Color Never Seen
for jjssa

eyelids closed
touch
moss without rock
honey without sticky sweetness
river feathers without fear
remember body surfing
in rhythm, attuned
to the preciousness
of time for love
listen to pulse beat
small wild crooning joy
lick salt tears
from the hardened jewel
smell warm almond-frangipani
essences blended
sink into stillness
punctuated by
mourning dove
feathered ear
silked thigh
feel the comfort
of known sensation
allow the heart

to flood
through a new song
to petals exuding oil
of a pure color
never seen

1982

Synesthesia Cycle II

Touch Dancing
For ADE

far from you in the familiar beauty
of this loved valley unknown to you
i smell your skin in newly washed green
your juices in magnolia and wild rose
hear the river sigh my name
in your muted undertone
low variations of the fugue
caressing rounded stone, roughly
smoothed like the heel of your hand
feel your breath in comforting air
softened by altitude and humidity
feared only in brief drafts of pain
between hills in evening and in wisps of
morning fog exposing pockets of doubt
soft air enclosing and nudging me
into light subdued as your gaze, into
gently loving rain on big-leafed
trees, layering sensation on sensation
until i am touch dancing with you
no sense of mystery or distance

1982

Synesthesia Cycle III

Crossword Dictionary

If I could spell
the sound of the river
would you smell its freshness?

If I could tell
the taste of hand-picked
raspberries warm from the sun
would you hear the seeds
crunch in your mouth?

If I could touch you
the way I want to be touched
would you know my memories?

If I could dance
the bubbles of new love
would you feel a caress?

If I could sing
my delight in the cardinals
would you perceive a vermillion
aura in a western tree?

If I could bake

my sadness into a biscuit
would you smell the sentiment
would it melt in your mouth?

1993

Memento

To GER

I wore a compass
for charting the unknown
You wore rings -- each
a bit of your history
and the compass, too, part
of mine -- my brother's
for scouting unfamiliar
areas I never ventured
into until now on this
boat with you, an
uncharted territory of
mirrored stillness
varied tides and rhythms
wild moments and
familiar landmarks
interspersed
crosshatched by
horizontal/diagonal waves
on the surface of
deep waters as yet
unfathomed

1981

Occasional Reflections

(Picnic at the San Francisco Palace of Fine Arts)

A glossy black duck
pushes along its
double, upside down
joined at the surface
A boy takes a girl's picture
as she poses
She snaps his as he
gives instructions
We, positioned at nether
ends of a mat beneath
the copper beech, see
eye to chestnut eye
as we unfold waxed-paper
wrappings, choose in
same order, alternate
sips of blanc de blancs
in view of the earthtoned
palace, clay and sand
where the muses turn
inward, gazing into the depths
seeking their own images
witnessing a cleansing
focusing on the eroticism
shimmering from our mat

unfolding a screen
of separate histories
while the Japanese wedding
party, as predicted, piles
from shiny cars, crosses
the busy street, composes
group shots by the pond
before the romantic setting
as if the city
had ceased to exist
We skirt pond edges
away from the central
projectory fountain
noisily shooting up foaming
white water that plummets down
We recognize our images
near the shallows
where leaves mysteriously
join in cloudy grey
and silver gelatin
shift and settle deep
into comfortable darkness
then, boundaries blurred
flash out again
nudging one another
toward clarity and repose

1981

Oh

I think of all I have found erotic . . .
the smell of mama's stockings in the bottom
       drawer
Lady Esther powder on grandmama's cheek
a lover's first electric touch
the forbidden: the sleazy motel
her employer's bed, the sand bar
in full view in the Russian River
fantasy, drama, the unexpected
romance: rose petals found between the sheets
the uncharacteristic move, tender or fierce
a steady rhythm   then a missed beat
the quality of skin, changing color
voice released, breath released
the sounds   oh, the sounds

1985

Crones' Way

for lir

From limerence to despair
and back through high desert
to rocky coasts of difference
with intermittent dips into
tubs of hot, deep sex
feelings hidden then exposed
passing as lovers, loving
passing as friends, caring
we clamber together again
across the barriers
meeting or missing
at halfway points
Duboce flat to Sonoma hills
children, empty hearts
busy minds, scars, lust
longing dragging us forward
so much baggage, so many
stories, reasons, restraints
finally bare truths, tears
and touch dissolve separateness
distant separateness

Hand-in-hand, crones now
on barely discernable paths
we transform ourselves
each other, the way

1988

Tipi

For DI
Ten-Mile, Mendocino

You had been jealous, angry
I, reserved, shut down
When you finally called
eager assent leapt up my throat
Awkward on the long drive
cautiously making conversation
my body began to melt toward
you, even before I relaxed
Our canoe pressed the ribbon
of the stream. Moon and
stars shot overhead, quick
and erratic as tiddlywinks
Horses plotted how to penetrate
the hedge around our campsite
The heavy aries sheep put her head
down, through gate to vulval entrance
made herself at home, blending
into your comforter, leaving only
when forced. The barn swallow
careened in and out of the fire circle
inviting me to fly with her
beautiful wings spread, all hungry intent
then wheeled abruptly, disappearing

perceived sharp as any blade
from the corner of my eye
But within the tipi, hooves and beaks
receded into the feather-smooth, lanolin-soft
reason for being alive in these bodies
on this ...in filtered light

1986

Seguras Otter

In therapy, the 3D
escher print of life
emerges, four, five
generations overlaid
flying fin to wing
connections disguised
in bare-branched trees
patterns swimming
feather by scale

identical twin rorschachs
individuated snowflakes
or tic tac toe?   perfect
for computers and lovers
of either/or solutions

stroking my hair, hand
cupped over my left ear, she
sighs, "*cherish and honor*"
half-hearing, half-guessing
"*seguras otter?*" I venture
incredulous, excited
"*yes*," she soothes, "*yes*"

1990

Morning Notes

My mind gets stuck
Behind white american dream pickets
Or old-fashioned hunter's green lattice
Though once I escaped by the back
Gate following a neon rainbow

> *Memory is a burden*
> *Or else,   all I am*

Gets trapped under the weeping mulberry
Within the wire and yew hedge
Where my daughters played
And I made an L-shaped flower garden
Varietals blooming cheek to cheek

> *In memory, there are only two*
> *Cardinal predictions from the red bird:*
> *"Pretty-day-pretty-day" or "Wet-wet-wet"*

Now, in Western twilight my gaze
Is riveted to the silent instinctive
Action of the Great Blue Heron
Whose voice I seldom hear above
The clattering clack of the young

In hard-won contemplation I root
Through layers of memory

I still shun compromise, a dirty word
Longing for exquisitely defined desire
To bond me with one who wants
Above all to make a home with me

Not to be stuck, trapped
Not to give up difference
Not to lose independence
No white picket fence
No lattice, wire or hedge

Above all to sustain a place of possibility
Four hands shaping the dream
Twined imaginations going to seed
Ripening into mysterious new color

1998

Amaryllis Belladonna

Late summer pink-fleshed
naked ladies flaunt tall
leafless bodies above
poisonous bulbs
in southern exposure
hardy and long-lived
through mild winters

Bare blossoms
rivet the attention
of alert passersby
more surely than
any bathing beauty

Lush clusters trumpet
from weedy roadsides
proclaiming pink
the color to celebrate
through late summer
the season of sheer joy

All praise to the nude
unexpected gift
from bare earth

2015

Cool

for nep

We meet. She's cool
We keep turning up at the same time.
I feel giddy whenever we talk.
One day she says "You're trouble."
"How come?" "You flirt." "So? You tease."
She gives me a look and a chocolate.
I go away for a long weekend.
When I get back, she's still cool.
I say "Last week I guess
you were just fooling around
but I need to tell you
when I flirt, I mean it."
Embarrassed, I raise my eyes
to meet her level gaze.
Without blinking, she replies
"So do I."

1993

Leftover Love

"There is a place the gain must go. The leftover love."
                              Alice Walker

After the first ending
leftover love is packed
tightly bound, stored
low in the deepfreeze

Love that once
expanded the world
warmed the heart
then wounds at every
touch to its icy shards

Years later, long after
an extended ending
deep frozen leftover
love suddenly exhumed
is still dangerous
smokes, gives off
the heat of dry ice
not quite creditable, yet
potent and alluring

Finally, leftover love
rounds and softens

razor-sharp edges
becomes mercifully fluid
leaving a reflecting pool
for new perspectives

2016

Seasonal Crisis

Just before holidays
and her birthdays
she is gripped by
a crisis of intention
examines her direction
turns to her journal
feels losses deeply
casts a critical eye
on our relationship
retreats into herself
before tackling the whirl
of celebration and
togetherness, travel
entertaining, giving
receiving and sharing

Only after serious focus
on the pro & con balance
sheet does she return
not, perhaps, confident
of ultimate goal but
willing once again to
take on the possibility
of joy, ease, connection
juggling demands and limitations

of resources, energy, bonds
of friendship and love
in all their contradictions
as another year passes

2008

Loss

"There is a place the loss must go"
                                    Alice Walker

light the snow
dark my love

          in these days

blue my mood
loss tossed to the violets
then on

          to compost

rich black fertile bed
needing tears to sprout
forced

          paper-whites

2013

Delicate Protections

Tomales Bay

here in the land of no seasons
all seasons conspiring to confuse
we wear both rawhide and silk
next to the skin for protection

redwood suckers rub branches
with golden rain trees
rolling hills are interrupted
> *only by a superimposed image*
> *of fences strung with barbed wire*
> *a small rectangular reflection*
> *from another perspective*
not the dominant vision

here the road, earthier than
O'Keefe's, like hers ends in mystery
not floating over the landscape
rather sunk deeply into ground
surface of hills mere hummocks
to lift off, rearrange like little
mounds of moss in a terrarium

how easily such transpositions
might take place in a life

how many choices there are
for the perceptive eye once
it rests from classifying
comparing, considering time
of year, once it allows itself
to caress the scene, move over
around, away, back again to
seeing, feeling the loved one

here limestone monoliths were
at once smoothed, rounded by
glacial movement and cracked
cratered, pocked, left with
great nipples erect, laced
in lichen, yellow, rust, green
grey, network of delicate
protections

1981

O'Keefe's Cliffs

from Ghost Ranch

Today the color of her famous
pink and yellow canyon cliffs

bordered by a troubled grey sky
blue- and yellow-green leaves

is tempered to seventy degrees
in a whirr of swallow wings

blends smoothly with adobe walls
pale beside cosmos and hollyhock

can hardly outdo the mosquito drone
or the softness of distant

more familiar mountains of blue

1996

Toward Winter Solstice

High tide in the wetlands
low in the world economy

Shortened days give way
to longer, darker nights

Despair for the state of the planet
teeters for balance with a hint of hope

A fragrant tree, a child's bright eyes
an old friend at ones' side give comfort
renew the effort to bring light to the early
night of the season

We sing to honor velvety darkness
drum, carol, and dance
recite beloved childhood rhymes
tell old, old stories, revive
dreams of a bright, safe, peaceful
circle of creatures of every kind ~
furred, feathered, finned, thick-
and thin-skinned, thousand-legged
and two ~ all under a full moon
longing equally for sun, rain and
sweet air to breathe together

the will to enjoy the blessings of
our shared earth, the possibility for
renewal in a silent night wind ~
regenerated vitality of life at
first light

2008/2009

Snow

a plump gobbet of snow
in the crotch of each tree
bushy dark green oaks
      in every hill's crack
an ultra absorbent pad
      between an elder's thighs
floods over the bank
      of hurricane battered levees
all familiar, nothing new
      thoughts and feelings recur
as my plane slices through
      clouds, making a new path
showing the circuitous way to
      coming day, fresh as frost
beautiful and risky alike
      innocent passion for life
present in low times as well as high
      draws me on, driving intent
seeking hidden desire somewhere
      in silent snowfall

2007

Northwest

for Wood, Van Zee + Knox clans

Red berry-laden trees
attract flocks of robins
jays, little brown jobbers
The family comes in, gathers
around holiday treats –
three kinds of pies, seven
traditional cookies, above all
salty Virginia country ham

Appetites sated, we lounge
around memory-tinged
Christmas décor, cards with
news and images of friends
scattered across the globe
heads grey, children grown
homes, careers, vacations touted
illness and loss barely mentioned

As the pink of evening fades
festive lights celebrating
winter solstice lure us out
again to stretch still limbs
under the no-name trees
We wonder what Northwest bird
harbors in the big nest above
our beloved neighborhood

2014

Epiphany

Trees still LED lit
we, not so much
though peace signs
continue to rise
as hope stutters on
Epiphany's revelations
are masked by fog
this early morn
yet may be intuited
in sudden sunset
Greetings and thanks
mailed, warmth remains
in narcissus' insistence
awakening all senses
Bitter wine adds tang
music soothes night along
Would that the New Year
let my words loose
slide my perceptions
onto waiting white papers

2013

Narcissus

Not yet budding
after a vermillion fall
of breath-taking splendor

She stands bare-limbed
longing for more than
a moss-furred vernal equinox

Straining against the glare
of a paper-white ceiling
she flexes hair-thin roots

Flings out untried ideas
wing-ed seeds from heartwood
waiting to find what she intends

1999

Freedom

Oh, Janis

Learning to go it alone
appreciate my own company
glad not to need to keep up
to wait or to negotiate
joint decision-making
I enjoy spur-of-the moment
choices, not feeling lonely
though the only thing I can see
now in the huge auditorium of
hundreds of people is the
still arm around the woman
sitting in front of me, the
hand gently patting her
shoulder – I sort of hate
the look of it but later when
the arm hugs her ardently
close around her neck, I
don't care anymore even as
Linda Tillery wails "I'm so
lonesome I could cry" (or
is it "die"?) – it's the steady
plaid-clad arm with its ever so
subtle caress that gets me

2013

Feelings

Where do they come from
these feelings
how trashy and beery
they are
folded into themselves
tightly as anemones
and squishy
or solid, spread
starfish arms making
grooves in the sand
while rainbow tears
bubble up through
tangles of kelp
promising the serenity of
pacific azure but
still agitated by
constant whitecaps
of creativity

1999

Stenosis

Meditation Before Surgery

In the passage leaving the heart
floats a three-chambered design
working away, thin as tissue

until, that is, it begins to harden
create more worries for everyone
trying to stay supple, to adapt

learn the hidden message
of aortic stenosis   hear the
narrowing valve's sound

speak of the past or the
future   of sweet mystery
or mortality's sure thing

while trying to set the elusive
murmur to music, perhaps with
a minor chord
    doubly diminished

2005

Bovinity

It's still July when
sudden red slashes
through the maple
willow's new green
goes yellow and gold

Only two months ago
she was falling, aging
greying before her time
breathlessly stilled
after a few slow steps

in mid-June the docs
opened her chest again
to work their bovine valve
replacement magic, re-
starting a strong heartbeat

As the season changes
so her energy and stride
joy in sleep and waking
watching and walking
toward a familiar self

2012

Mortality

The seer can no more
know her own fate
than that of the earth
or the passing creek
but there are signs

Aches and pains join
alarming loss of acuity
senses, focus, memory
heavy breathing uphill
clicking knees coming
down, precarious
balance midstream
less willingness to risk
a fall, a relationship

Ignoring these hints
she dreams of revitalizing
long-abandoned projects
Ideas flitter around her
ricochet at dusk and dawn
settle at mid-day, fade
before the tv are gone
by the witching hour
leaving faintest lines
on her unread palm

2016

Needed: Tsunami Relief

Can a poem carry relief
beyond the page
open another heart or two
enlarge the pool
of compassion on which
we float together
hold the missing in memory
boost the courage of survival
memorialize lives lost
join sorrow to sorrow
across continents with
the long reach of word
to word, respect difference
share the challenge
of simply being human
in an imperfect world
waiting for relief

2018

House

She dreams
a gingerbread house
all angles and
shapenote windows

From ancient
Mennonite hymnals
and Russian
folk dances

She fills the
root cellar
with spiced
rainbow trout

'Til they flood
the skylight
to salmonberry
reality

1999

Spring Equinox

Warm hands massage
me deep into myself
Cool fingers raise
joy from within

Fire & comfort food
sweet talk, reading
rest mind and heart

I dream a Native
American journey
to many rivers
through a tree's
vulval opening

I receive a feather
a new flame
to take home
across the bridge
South to North
at the foot of the
mountain
between East and West

Sheltered by redwoods

I, once had long-hair
am always attuned
to a Cherokee braid
of fierce and gentle
winds

When I wake
I'm still warm

2017

Outing

Ah, lead me to a swinging
bridge over the creek
of my legacy, hold hands
as we cross, leaving angst
and conversation behind
watching dead leaves
of guilt float downstream
while the softness of skin
to skin comforts and
a silent heron in flight
beckons

2016

I Spy

I spy on the herons
The heron chicks, the fledglings
Their cousins & neighbors
I observe their daily activities
And imagine that I know them
But what about their
Secret lives? Their awareness
their instinct, their desire
Beyond my anthropomorphic rag
What mysteries would they reveal
If I could relate to them
One animal spirit to another
Seeing that my human

Filters hide, hearing sounds
Beyond my ears' ken, smells
More delicate than human sense
Softness & sharpness too dangerous
For me, tastes so delicious
My mouth waters at the thought
Of what I might perceive
If only I could

1998

Moment From My Eightieth Birthday Celebration

Anthem

Café guitarist
many-versed Hallelujah
I join the chorus

Pod

Distant puffs, backs, tails
pod of exhalation – my
exhilaration

Surprise

Seeking sea otters
one or two maybe? – No, threes
whole family rafts

Afternoon

No one in the pool
fenced flower garden spa

relaxing quiet

Toasts

Bubbly & bourbon
newly legal absinthe with
fresh elderberry flower

Nepenthe

Driftwood phoenix reigns
open fire-pit logs blaze red
breeze cools as sun sets

Reward

Uphill, trekking poles
steadily pull me forward
despite facing wind

Bald eagle riffs ~ o-
ver cliff, feathers ruffled
clutches prey and me

2013

Comet

Always another day
to catch a sunset
but the passing comet
a rarity sought and chased
all week, today thrills
appearing as predicted
a big snowfall with a tall
shooting down, turning
pink with the setting sun
soon visible only through
binoculars and fast fading
as the earth turns and I
become eighty

2013

Short Days

By fall, I emerge, hungry, full
of energy, determined, skipping the cracks
toward what I love, pristine lined
tablet and pencil in hand, oxfords
tightly laced, bookbag swinging by my side
repeatedly going the distance
new knowledge to known comfort
hardly aware of dangerous crossings

Scared and excited, rushing toward
acknowledgement of All Hallows, all that
is known to be dead mixed with outrageous
possibility ~ surprises, disguises, make-believe
switched identity, utter exposure in hiddenness
mop-headed lions and switched-on carton
automatons
daymares realized and made flesh, dancing
hooting, bag-carrying portents from the grave

For the holidays, I latch onto new and old
loved ones as if they can count on me
to be "home" in all our forms ~ pumpkin to
turkey, filled stocking to Auld Lang Syne
and one kiss at the countdown

1986

70

Late Winter

Shenandoah Valley

Willow branches sway
leaves still attached
speaking, trying to say…
something new, I suppose
wrestling with one another
like discarded wads
of tracing paper
wrinkling, refusing
to die in the trash
hanging on
like Spanish moss
saying, saying why they
failed this year to turn soft
and golden, coursing to earth
in moist shimmering cascades

Hush! Hush, willow leaves
You're dead and must fall
despite the tinge of green
in your grey
You must be shaken into
a basket and hauled away
to a place where
there is neither sighing nor speaking

The wind is compelling the willow
to let down her leaves
at last

1972

Free Range

Now, I'm an old woman
free-ranging belly & thighs
breasts and desire
judging everyone younger
ridiculously raw & untried
each older woman a risk
a reminder, denial shattered

Fragile, we lie in a bed of
rose petals, soft, precious
drifting onto my heart, strings
attached as to a gifted heirloom
carrying significance & stories
from other lives, other times
greedily embracing this day
before learning to let go

1997

The Greats

Groundhog Day in the City Again

Urban wildness still thrives here
the great blue heron claims a nest in
the center thrilling me and miz mole
out of the blahs we ogle the big bird
daily and circle the lake looking
for a night heron or a horned owl
something rare hardly glancing at
squat flocks of gulls ducks juncos
commoners of the park wondering
why tall thin unique so cherished
sought after immortalized in art
while ordinary existence goes unsung
or destroyed at home along with
poisoned rodents and hardy pigeons
barely discouraged by unwelcoming
barbs glues chemicals fake raptors

Still doves mourn beautifully finches
& sparrows feed above fat cats secretive
squirrels and masked bandits at dusk
so much insistent life despite fierce
storms and constant traffic mere yards
from swift iridescent hummers over
intersecting tracks of vanished snails

glistening in morning sun catching my
eye as I make coffee and scones to tame
the news soothe the heart build strength
for another day of simply being a person
in a complex tangle of reasons and
necessities that yet leave open the
choice to walk 'round a golden gate
island and pause in awe beside a great
white egret wading fishing watching
before I slog through mud and ennui
toward not greatness but life exposed
by the groundhog's shadow to a season
of unreliable weather before the
promise of an ever-renascent spring

1996/1997

Abandon

How I long to let loose
be giddy as a peony
carefree and full of humor
as a fledging kookaburra
unembarrassed to be
common as a laughing

gull, witty as any
rhyming fool unafraid

of deep dark waters
facing naked old truths
hang-gliding without a net
swooping down dunes
to collect more and more
shells, rocks, feathers
friends and lovers
without a blush

2016

Author's Notes

Ida VSW Red Creative Resume

Archives

Author's Notes

"Groundhog Day in the City"
"I'm ole miz mole
And I live in a hole
Bless my soul
Love this hole that I live in!"*
*folk version from traditional children's song.

"Nursery Rhyme"
WPA: Work Projects Administration, 1935-1943,
Franklin Roosevelt's "New Deal" job creation.

"They Met"
Roundtable prompt 7-28-16 from Martha Rosalis
poem Mavericks. "The body spoke first. Then the
fear."

"Peace on May Day"
Performed with Mothertongue Feminist Theater
Collective in "Women in the Peace Movement " and
featured in an oil painting by Mary Angela Collins.

"Synesthesia Cycle 2, Touch Dancing"
Performed with Mothertongue Feminist Theater
Collective in "Loving Women".

Published in New Lesbian Writing, edited by
Margaret Cruikshank, San Francisco: Grey Fox, 1984.

"Synesthesia Cycle 3, Crossword Dictionary"
Ida VSW Red with Mothertongue Feminist Theater
Collective script group.
Performed with Mothertongue Feminist Theater
Collective in "Lesbian Erotica".

"Memento"
Published in UCSF Synapse Literary Issue Vol. 29,
No. 30, May 23, 1985.

"Occasional Reflections"
Performed with Mothertongue Feminist Theater
Collective in "Loving Women".

"Oh"
Read at the Lesbian Erotica Reading organized by Pat
Saliba at Old Wives Tales.
and performed with Mothertongue Feminist Theater
Collective in "Loving Women " & "Lesbian Erotica".

"Crones' Way"
Performed with Mothertongue Feminist Theater
Collective in "Lesbian Erotica," "Loving Women,"
and "Speaking of Aging". Limerence (psychology) – a
state of mind resulting from romantic attraction,

characterized by feelings of euphoria, the desire to have one's feelings reciprocated, etc.

"Cool"
Performed with Mothertongue Feminist Theater Collective in "Lesbian Erotica".

"Delicate Protections"
Published in New Lesbian Writing, edited by Margaret Cruikshank. 1980: San Francisco. CA: Grey Fox, 1985.

"Narcissus"
Written in GLOE Women Writers Group. Read in Martha Courtot's reading at Cotati Women's Library. See drawing in "Workshop -- GLOE [Operation Concern's Gay and Lesbian Outreach to Elders - ed.]" folder.

"Feelings"
Written in GLOE Women Writers Group, facilitated by Martha Courtot.
"I Spy"
Written in Women Writers Group, Gay & Lesbian Outreach to Elders.

"Short Days"
Fragment of my "Sixth Season".

Ida VSW Creative Resume

This resume gathers an incomplete compendium of Ida's educational and creative activities. Everything listed here was something of importance to her and many were sources of great personal satisfaction and pride.

Education

B.A. in English with minor in drama.
Mary Baldwin College, 1954
Courses in Shakespeare, Jacobian drama, French
dramatists, modern dramatists, production, direction,
and speech.

Tulane University, 1957
Graduate study of Shakespeare

M.A. in English
University of Virginia, 1973
Thesis on the poetry of W. S. Merwin. Minor
emphasis on contemporary drama, especially the
absurdists.

M.S. in Library Science
Catholic University, 1976
Emphasis on poetry therapy.

Training and Workshops

Numerous writing groups and workshops

Frameline Generations Film Workshop

Theater workshops with:
> Helen Stotzfus of A Traveling Jewish Theatre
> Geraldine Baron of New York Actors Studio
> Mimi Gina of American Art Theatre
> Donna Davis of Theater Rhinoceros

Writing for performance workshops with:
> Irene Fornes
> Michele Linfante
> Helen Stoltzfus
> Anna Deavere Smith

Lesbian Feminist Publications

Contributor of essay *Naming
The Lesbian Path*,
edited by Margaret Cruikshank.
(San Francisco. Grey Fox, rev. ed. 1985)

Poetry editor
Contributor of poems *delicate protections* and *touch
dancing*
New Lesbian Writing,
edited by Margaret Cruikshank.
(San Francisco. Grey Fox, 1984)

Author of "Note on 'Reading a Subject' in Periodical
Indexes",
Lesbian Studies,
edited by Margaret Cruikshank.
(Old Westbury, NY. Feminist Press, 1982)

Numerous poems published in *Synapse*, the student
newspaper of the University of California, San
Francisco (1985-1994). Searchable in the UCSF
archive at synapse.library.ucsf.edu/

Additional credits in *Entre Nous: Between Us, A
Newsmagazine for Lesbians* and publications of the
UCSF Women's Resource Center, GLOE (New Leaf

Gay & Lesbian Outreach to Elders), and OLOC (Old Lesbians Organizing for Change.

Selected List of Reading Venues

UCSF Women's Center

Valencia Rose

Modern Times

Old Wives Tales

GLOE

Feminist Writers Guild

KALX

SF Public Library

LGBT Center

The Redwoods

Contributions to *Sinister Wisdom:*
A multicultural lesbian literary & art journal

Lynn Brown contributed an obituary for Ida. (Issue 219, Winter 2021)

Poem *Free Range* and interview of Jess McVey. (Issue 78/79, Winter 2009/2010)

Review of the book *Shedding Grace and Other Stories* by Mab Maher. (Issue 77, Fall 2009)

Fiction *The Mauvety*. (Issue 72, Winter 2007)

Poem *Sister Mothertongue* and co-author of 30th anniversary history of Mothertongue Feminist Theater Collective. (Issue 70, Spring 2007)

Poem *A Celebration of Women Who Work* and narrative
Help Wanted.
(Issue 67, Summer 2006)

Poems *Autumn* and *The Greats: Groundhog Day in the
City Again.*
(Issue 63, Winter 2004)

Poems *One Sentence* and *Lesbian Feminist Analysis.*
(Issue 62, Summer 2004)

Essay *Seasoning*, in *Old Lesbians/Dykes*, a special
journal issue co-edited by Ida VSW Red as a member
of a collective of nine lesbians over the age of 60.
(Issue 53, Summer/Fall 1994)

Mothertongue Feminist Theater Collective

As a founding member of what was first known as Mothertongue Reader's Theater, Ida wrote for and acted in more than 20 original scripts. These deeply personal and political creations were collectively staged and produced in over ninety performances at a variety of local and statewide venues.

Themed scripts included:

Anger	Celebrating Women
Breasts and Roses	Survival
Body Talk	Women and Peace
Women and Rape	Still Angry
Food	Lesbian Games
Sex Roles	Eat Rice
Work	Adoption and Surrender
Transits	Speaking of Ageing
Mothers and Daughters	Lesbian Erotica
Loving Women	Sisters
Passing	

Ida also composed *Mothertongue Feminist Theater Collective: The First Twenty Years, 1976-1996, An Index* (Available in the Mothertongue archive)

Ida edited the collective's *Mothertongue Handbook* in 1993.
(Available at: mothertonguefeministtheater.org/)

California Theater

Alice in *Smell* by Sandy Steinman (Steve North, Dir.), "Fringe of Marin" Festival of New Bay Area One-Act Plays and Solo Performances, Dominican University & Community (2002)

Ensemble, *The Vagina Monologues*, San Francisco State University (1999)

Pat Bond in *Scenes From Her Life and Performances*, Gay & Lesbian Outreach to Elders, Pat Bond Awards Ceremony (1994)

Jean in *Road to Mecca* by Athol Fugard and Charlie in Omega by E. Coulsan Hall, rehearsed scenes, Brava for Women in the Arts Workshop (1989)

Mrs. Culhill in *Leaving Joe* by Sheila Ganz, rehearsed reading, ExiTheatre (1989)

Granny Blue in *Living on Salvation Street* by Terry Garner, rehearsed reading, Studio, Theatre Rhinoceros (1984)

Babe in *Possessions* by Terry Garner, People's School of Dramatic Arts (1983)

Peter in *The Leaves Were Full of Children* by Carmen de Monteflores, rehearsed reading, Valencia Rose (1983)

Anna III in *Who Done It?* by Susan Yankowitz, Studio Eremos (1982)

East Coast Theater (1950s-1970s)

Oak Grove Theater, Verona, VA
As an original member of Oak Grove, a summer subscription theater at director Fletcher Collins' Pennyroyal Farm, played supporting roles and leads, including:

- Madame Rosepettle in *Oh Dad, Poor Dad* . . .
- Amanda Wingfield in *The Glass Menagerie*
- Ruth in *Blithe Spirit*
- Candida in *Candida*
- Rosabel in *Venus Observed*
- Mrs. Clandon in *You Never Can Tell*
- Mary Hallen in *Who's Happy Now*
- Lady Chiltern in *An Ideal Husband*
- Sabrina in *Sabrina Fair*

Theater Wagon, Staunton, VA
As an original member of Theater Wagon, a traveling troupe of playwrights, actors, and directors dedicated to producing new plays, medieval revivals, and translations, played supporting roles and leads, including:

- Belle in *Lady and the Unicorn* by Margaret Collins
- Rose in *Yaqui* by Barbara Allen
- Nurse Irina in *Ship of the Righteous* by Nicolai Evreinov, translated by C. Collins

Valley Players, Harrisonburg, VA
As a founding member of Valley Players, a community theater, played supporting roles and leads, including:

- Sarah in *J. B.*

- Louise in *Five Finger Exercise*
- Mary in *The Women*
- Penelope Sycamore in *You Can't Take It with You*

New Orleans Little Theater, New Orleans, LA
- Claudia in *Claudia*

Mary Baldwin College (Staunton, VA)
- Mary Magdalene in *Family Portrait*
- Pierrot in *Aria da Capo*
- Mrs. Phelps in *The Silver Cord*
- Mother in *Sweetmeat Game*
- The Sphinx in *The Infernal Machine*

Directorial Credits

Blood Lines, by Carmen de Monteflores, Rio Loiza Productions at Brava! for Women in the Arts, San Francisco, CA, 1994

Bridgewater College, Bridgewater, VA
The Grass Harp, *Pygmalion*, *The Oaks of Mamre*

Valley Players, Harrisonburg, VA
The Curious Savage, *The American Dream*, *The Sandbox*,

Oak Grove Acorns, Verona, VA
The Emperor's New Clothes,

Mary Baldwin College, Staunton, VA
The Madwoman of Chaillot, *The Silver Cord*

Film & Television Projects

Seniors Rocking, a documentary short about the creation of a performance piece that the American dance pioneer Anna Halprin created in Marin County in 2005. Ida is a featured participant in the 2010 film. (vimeo.com/401366259)

Changeling: A Lesbian-Feminist Fable, a film by Ida VSW Red, Frameline Generations Workshop (2008)

Old Dyle in *& All That Jazz*, a Frameline Generations Workshop production (2008)

Ensemble, *Sisterspeak*, Mothertongue performance for Gayble TV, Channels 26/28/29 (2002)

Cast, *Festival Trailer*, San Francisco International Lesbian & Gay Film Festival (1999)

Professional Publications

Coordinating Editor, Health Policy and Nursing: Crisis and Reform in the U.S. Health Care Delivery System, edited by Charlene Harrington & Carroll L. Estes (Boston, MA. Jones and Bartlett, 1994)

Editor, Long Term Care Crisis: Elders Trapped in a No-Care Zone, by Carroll L. Estes, James H. Swan, & Associates (Newbury Park, CA. Sage, 1993)

Editor & Designer, Cost of Smoking in California, by Dorothy P. Rice & Wendy Max (Sacramento, CA. California Department of Health Services, 1992)

Contributing Editor, The Nation's Health, edited by Philip R. Lee & Carroll L. Estes. (Boston. Jones and Bartlett, 3rd ed., 1990)

Editor, Designer, and Desktop Publisher, Cost of Injury in the United States, by Dorothy P. Rice, Ellen J. MacKenzie, & Associates (Atlanta, GA. U.S. Centers for Disease Control, 1989)

Coordinating Editor, Serving the Mentally Ill Elderly: Problems and Perspectives, by Elinore E. Lurie, James H. Swan, & Associates (Lexington, MA: Lexington/Heath, 1987)

Compiler of "Resources," Women Take Care: The Consequences of Caregiving in Today's Society, by Tish Sommers, Laurie Shields, & The Older Women's League (Gainesville, FL. Triad, 1987)

Coordinating Editor, Long Term Care of the Elderly: Public Policy Issues, by Charlene Harrington, Robert J. Newcomer, Carroll L. Estes, & Associates (Beverly Hills, CA. Sage, 1985)

Editor and Producer of Institute for Health & Aging newsletters, brochures, & promotional flyers (1978-1992)

Archives

Ida's writing and personal papers are preserved in the archives of the James C. Hormel LGBTQIA Center of the San Francisco Public Library. As of this publication date, cataloging is still underway. For information or access to archive materials, email sfhistory@sfpl.org.

Ida's large collection of books was also received by the San Francisco Public Library, for accession to the collection or dispersal to other libraries.

A 2-hour interview with Ida was conducted by Arden Eversmeyer in March, 2003 as part of the Old Lesbian Oral Herstory Project. Ida interviewed several subjects as well. This project resides in the Sophia Smith Collection of Women's History at Smith College. Interviews can be located by searching findingaids.smith.edu. Transcripts and digital audio files can be requested via email at specialcollections@smith.edu.

Digital archives of *Sinister Wisdom* are available as downloadable PDF files at sinisterwisdom.org/ArchiveThe

Mothertongue history and current activity can be found at https://mothertonguefeministtheater.org/. A Mothertongue archive is composed of scripts, "Extra Pieces" (writing not included in scripts), newsletters, flyers, administrative files, photographs, and various audio-visual materials that reflect the activities of this women's theater group that began in

1976, and were still active when they donated the collection in 1999 is housed in the GLBT Historical Society Archives. The collection can be searched at www.glbthistory.org/catalog-search.

www.ingramcontent.com/pod-product-compliance
Lightning Source LLC
Chambersburg PA
CBHW020753130626
46554CB00006B/2172